Yogi

THE LIFE, LOVES, AND LANGUAGE OF
BASEBALL LEGEND YOGI BERRA

BARB ROSENSTOCK

Illustrated by **TERRY WIDENER**

CALKINS CREEK
AN IMPRINT OF HIGHLIGHTS
Honesdale, Pennsylvania

Lawdie Berra loved . . .

His family—Mom, Pop, Tony, Mike, John, and baby Josie.

His Italian neighborhood, *La Montagna,* "The Hill," in St. Louis, Missouri.

His friends.

Sports.

Lawdie Berra did not love . . . school.
When neighbors asked, "How do you like school?"
Lawdie answered, "Closed."

Lawdie made people laugh, but he wasn't trying to be funny, just honest. Later, he was known for the way he talked. But in the 1930s, folks on The Hill knew him as a short, big-nosed, funny-looking kid—one of the neighborhood boys who went *pazzo!*—crazy—for baseball.

"WE WERE OVERWHELMING UNDERDOGS." —Yogi

Lawdie and his friends borrowed gloves and baseballs. They nailed splintered bats together and turned old magazines into shin guards. At an abandoned clay-mine dump, the guys hauled away broken bottles, outlined a diamond, and dragged in two rusted cars for dugouts. They called their team the Stags, joined local leagues, and beat most teams in the city.

"WHEN YOU COME TO A FORK
IN THE ROAD, TAKE IT." —Yogi

Storeowners on The Hill wouldn't pay for the Stags' uniforms; baseball was "a bum's game." Lawdie's older brothers had been offered major league tryouts, but Pop stopped that nonsense and insisted they get real jobs. Now that Lawdie wanted to play baseball instead of going to high school, his brothers helped him beg for a chance until their parents said, *sì*—yes.

Lawdie and his friend Joey Garagiola joined an American Legion travel team. Lawdie started catching. He worked regular jobs, too—selling newspapers, wrapping coal blocks, driving a soda truck. Most days, he carried a mitt and left early to play ball. The jobs never lasted.

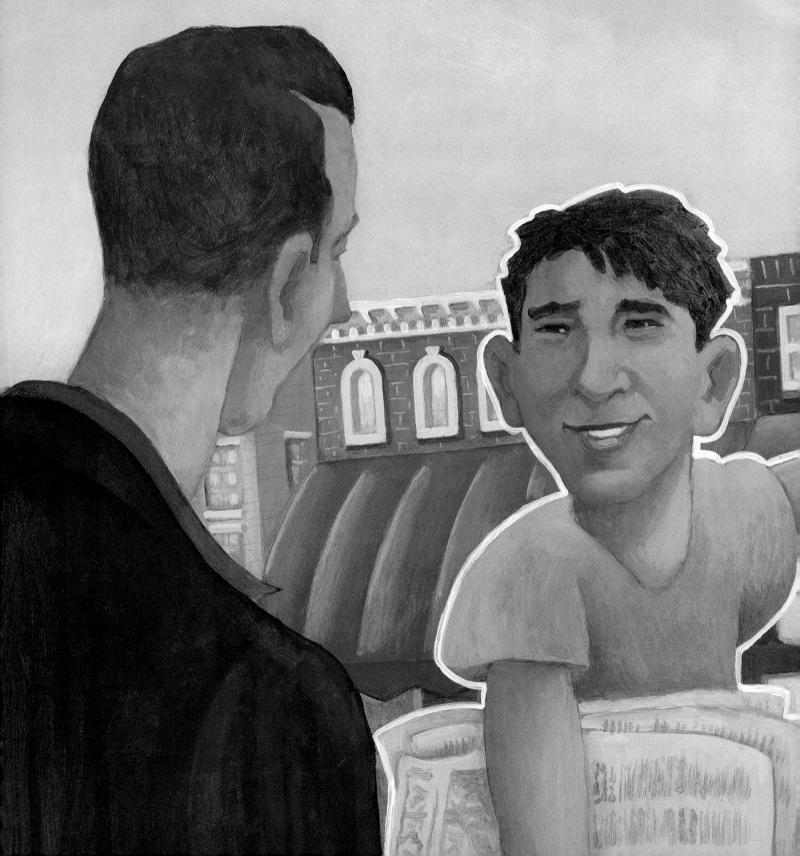

"YOU CAN OBSERVE A LOT
BY WATCHING." —Yogi

Lawdie loved his coaches. But coaches didn't always love him back. *Wait for a good pitch! Don't slide like that! You're gonna fall over, Berra!* He took a lot of teasing for his squat body, long arms, and waddling walk. When he wasn't on the field, Lawdie studied the game from the sidelines with his arms and legs crossed. After his friends saw a movie where a yogi sat cross-legged and charmed snakes, Lawdie was called "Yogi."

Yogi smashed the ball and tore around the bases—much faster than he looked. Though he played all wrong, it turned out all right. His American Legion team made the national playoffs two years in a row. The St. Louis Cardinals asked Yogi and Joey to try out for the majors!

Yogi loved his hometown team. But the Cardinals didn't love him back. They offered Joey a contract but said Yogi looked too clumsy to play in the big leagues.

Yogi watched his friend head to the major leagues while he pulled tacks in a shoe factory. He played semipro pickup games to make a few bucks and still loved, loved, loved baseball. But would baseball ever love him back?

NOTHING." —Yogi

"IF THE WORLD WERE PERFECT,

In 1942, a scout offered Yogi a spot on a New York Yankees minor league team. But he played only one season before World War II broke out. So baseball had to wait.

Yogi enlisted in the Navy and fought as a gunner's mate, protecting soldiers landing on the shore. *Keep your head down, Berra!*

IT WOULDN'T BE." —Yogi

When the war ended, Yogi returned to the minor leagues in Newark, New Jersey. He caught and hit like a champion and moved one step closer to playing in New York.

On September 22, 1946, Yogi Berra played his first major league game. He smacked a two-run homer 340 feet into the stands at Yankee Stadium. Game after game, Yogi kept hitting. At first, he loved seeing his name in the papers. But the papers didn't always love him back.

Sportswriters called him pudgy, homely, and clown. They joked—*Yogi's so ugly he looks better with the catcher's mask on.*

His teammates called him caveman, freak, and Neanderthal.

Opposing players jeered—"What tree did you sleep in last night, Yogi?" One made Yogi "captain of the All-time All-America Ugly Team." Another hung from the dugout roof, scratched his underarms, and hooted like a monkey.

But these words hurt most: "He doesn't even look like a Yankee." New York Yankees were tall, handsome, and elegant. Who would want Yogi's face on a baseball card?

"IT'S NOT TOO FAR, IT JUST SEEMS LIKE IT IS." —Yogi

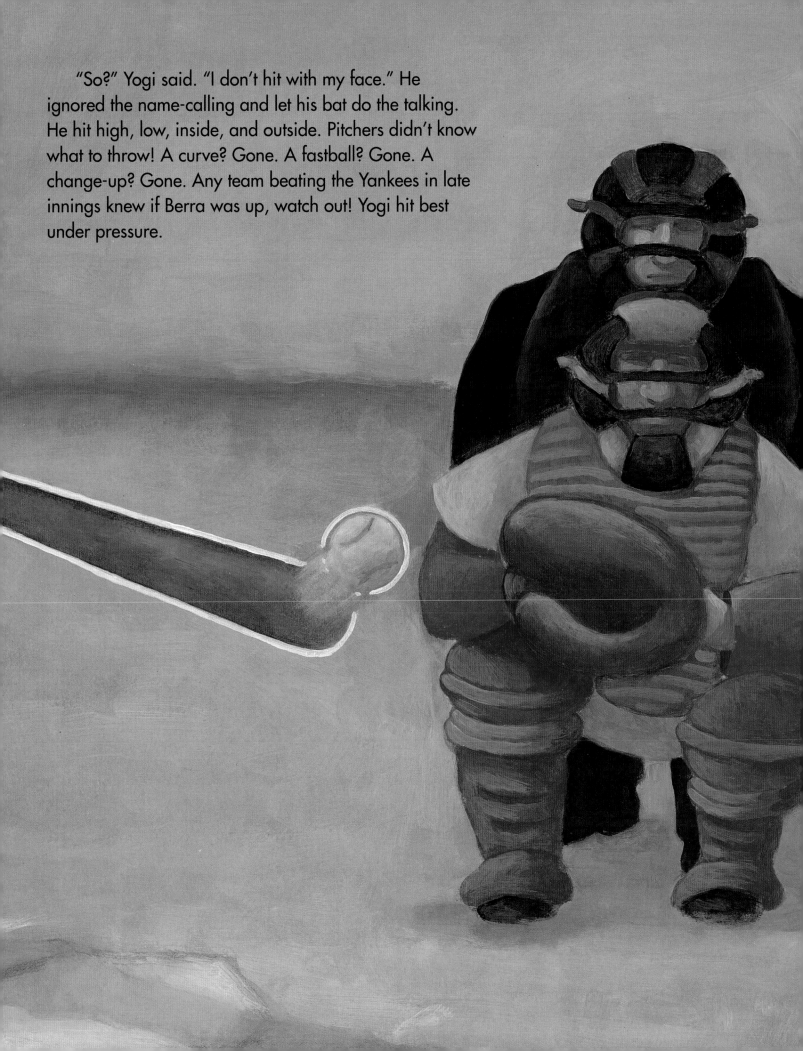

"So?" Yogi said. "I don't hit with my face." He ignored the name-calling and let his bat do the talking. He hit high, low, inside, and outside. Pitchers didn't know what to throw! A curve? Gone. A fastball? Gone. A change-up? Gone. Any team beating the Yankees in late innings knew if Berra was up, watch out! Yogi hit best under pressure.

"WE MADE TOO MANY WRONG MISTAKES." —Yogi

Yogi loved catching. But his pitchers didn't always love him
back. In his first few seasons, he dropped balls, threw wild. Runners
stole bases. Pitchers couldn't see Yogi's short fingers flashing signs.
He tried painting his nails; pitchers still shook him off.

In 1949, he worked with a retired catcher during spring training. *Squat closer! Frame that pitch! Step, then throw!* After months of practice, Yogi took charge, shifting fielders, calming pitchers, keeping umpires on their toes. Home plate became like Yogi's living room—he talked to everyone there and no one came in unless he let them.

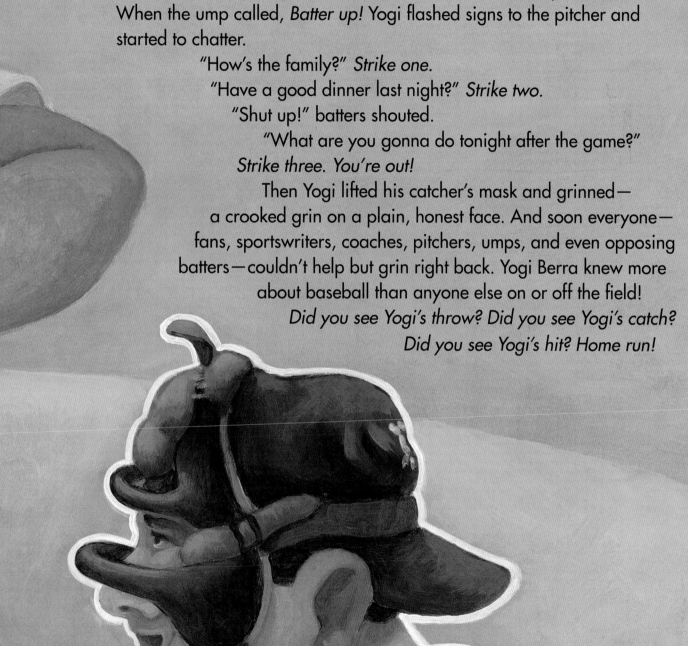

"HOW CAN YOU THINK AND HIT AT THE SAME TIME?" —Yogi

Yogi loved figuring out batters. But batters didn't always love him back. When the ump called, *Batter up!* Yogi flashed signs to the pitcher and started to chatter.

"How's the family?" *Strike one.*

"Have a good dinner last night?" *Strike two.*

"Shut up!" batters shouted.

"What are you gonna do tonight after the game?" *Strike three. You're out!*

Then Yogi lifted his catcher's mask and grinned— a crooked grin on a plain, honest face. And soon everyone— fans, sportswriters, coaches, pitchers, umps, and even opposing batters—couldn't help but grin right back. Yogi Berra knew more about baseball than anyone else on or off the field!

Did you see Yogi's throw? Did you see Yogi's catch?

Did you see Yogi's hit? Home run!

WORLD CHAMPIONS
1960
CHAMPIONS
WORLD CHAMPIONS
CHAMPIONS
CHAMPIONS
LEAGUE

"IT'S NEVER HAPPENED
        IN WORLD SERIES HISTORY,
        AND IT HASN'T HAPPENED SINCE." —Yogi

Between 1947 and 1963, Yogi's Yankees won the American
League pennant fourteen times. He earned a World Series ring for
each finger, more than any other player in history! He played nineteen
seasons in the majors and was named MVP three times. He met
celebrities, presidents, and the Pope. "Hello, Yogi!" "Hello, Pope!"

All people, famous or not, loved Yogi's way with words. "It's so crowded nobody goes there anymore." "If you can't imitate him, don't copy him." "It's déjà vu all over again." People quoted his Yogi-isms in speeches, newspapers, magazines, books, and on TV. His popular sayings were a lot like Yogi—simple, honest, funny, and wise.

"IT AIN'T OVER
TILL IT'S OVER." —Yogi

When his playing days passed, Yogi still loved baseball. And baseball loved him back. He coached or managed for twenty-nine more years. Yogi knew how to help young players. *Believe in yourself. Ignore the chatter. Work hard.* And never forget, "It ain't over till it's over."

Yogi Berra's love for baseball was never over.
The boy from The Hill loved sports, his friends, teammates,
and family his entire life. And the whole world, inside
baseball and out, loved his fearless heart, his fierce drive,
and his famous words. Always.

> "YOU'VE GOT TO BE CAREFUL IF YOU DON'T KNOW WHERE YOU'RE GOING BECAUSE YOU MIGHT NOT GET THERE." —Yogi

AUTHOR'S NOTE

Yogi Berra has been called "the greatest catcher who ever lived." He played on fourteen New York Yankees World Series teams, coached and managed for both the Yankees and the New York Mets, then finished his career as a coach with the Houston Astros. The small, odd-looking kid, whose neighborhood team played in plain white T-shirts, wound up wearing a coveted major league uniform for forty-three years, from 1946 until 1989.

Berra was born Lorenzo Pietro (Lawrence Peter) on May 12, 1925, to immigrants Pietro and Paolina Berra in a primarily Italian St. Louis neighborhood. His mother had a difficult time saying *Lawrence* in English, so she pronounced his name "Lawdie." Berra became known by that name throughout childhood. He was teased for his name, his looks, his lack of schooling, his speech, and how he ran, threw, caught, and hit, too. On the baseball field, the teasing turned into years of hazing. People called him so many names, so often, that it's become impossible to figure out who insulted Yogi first. When he was much older, Yogi admitted how much people's words had hurt him. But early on, a coach told him to ignore the comments and play hard. Yogi took that advice to heart.

Yogi Berra stood about five feet, eight inches tall. In team photos, he is dwarfed by classic Yankee ballplayers like Joe DiMaggio and Mickey Mantle. Yet Yogi led the NY Yankees in RBIs for seven consecutive seasons, from 1949 to 1955. Berra's big style of play, his friendliness, and his enthusiasm for the game won over the baseball world. Even in the minors, Yogi was a great hitter, though he drove coaches crazy swinging at bad balls. But Berra was a weak major league catcher until retired Yankee Hall of Famer Bill Dickey drilled him day after day in the fine points of the position. "Within two years, Yogi Berra will be the best catcher in the American League," Dickey said early in 1949. Yogi worked so hard, it was true by the end of that season. The best description of Yogi behind the plate comes from the famous Yankees manager, Casey Stengel, "He's out there behind the plate saying hello to everybody in sight. Oh, Mr. Berra is a very sociable fellow. He acts like home plate is his room."

Berra participated in a record twenty-one World Series as player, coach, or manager, winning thirteen times. He holds World Series records for the most games, at bats, hits, doubles, singles, games caught, and catcher putouts. He was behind the plate when Jackie Robinson stole home in the 1955 Series, but Yogi famously disputed the ump's call that day (and forever after) insisting, "He's still out." Berra caught the only perfect game in World Series history, Don Larsen's no-hitter against the Brooklyn Dodgers in 1956. Yogi was a fifteen-season All-Star and is one of only five players to be named MVP three times. In 1972, Lawrence Peter "Yogi" Berra was elected to the National Baseball Hall of Fame and to the All-Century Team in 1999.

Even though he could be shy and didn't like public speaking, Yogi had a lot to say about baseball and life. Berra has been quoted so often, by so many people, in so many places, that there is a special name for his sayings: "Yogi-isms." He's the most quoted athlete in *Bartlett's Familiar Quotations* and among the most quoted Americans of all time.

One of the best things about Yogi is how much he loved his family. He married Carmen Short in St. Louis in 1949. They had three athletically talented sons, who all played minor or major league baseball, and eleven grandchildren. They celebrated their sixty-fifth wedding anniversary before Carmen passed away in 2014, followed by Yogi on September 22, 2015, exactly sixty-nine years after his first game in the major leagues. Yogi was posthumously awarded the Presidential Medal of Freedom, the nation's highest civilian honor, for his integrity, military service, and commitment to civil rights, charity, and education.

Boyhood friends Joe Garagiola, a catcher for the St. Louis Cardinals, and Yogi Berra, a catcher for the New York Yankees

In Game 5 of the 1956 World Series, New York Yankee pitcher Don Larsen threw a perfect game against the Brooklyn Dodgers. In this famous photo, teammate Yogi Berra jumps into Larsen's arms.

YOGI'S AMAZING NUMBERS

CAREER STATS

Games: 2,120

R	H	2B	3B	HR	RBI	SB	BB	AVG	OBP	SLG
1,175	2,150	321	49	358	1,430	30	704	.285	.348	.482

World Series Records

Games Played: 75

Plate Appearances: 295

At Bats: 259

Hits: 71

Doubles: 10

Singles: 49

Games Caught: 63

Catcher Putouts: 457

A STRONG CATCHER, YOGI BERRA . . .

caught the only perfect game in World Series history, October 8, 1956.

had zero errors in the 88 games of the 1958 season.

caught at least 100 games in 10 seasons and caught both games of 117 doubleheaders.

led the American League in games caught for 7 straight years (1950–1956).

threw out 49 percent of potential base stealers, third-best in Major League Baseball history.

had a career fielding percentage of .988.

WOULD STAND
UNTIL IT WAS BROKEN." —Yogi

A POWER HITTER, YOGI BERRA . . .

hit the first pinch-hit home run in World Series history, in 1947.

batted an average of .314 with runners in scoring position between 1950 and 1956.

had two 30-home-run seasons (1952 and 1956) and eleven 20-home-run seasons.

drove in 80 runs in 11 consecutive seasons.

had 5 seasons with more home runs than strikeouts.

played his best season in 1954 with a .307 average, 22 home runs, and 125 runs batted in (RBI).

has the most career RBIs of any catcher, 1,430.

ONE OF THE GREATEST TO PLAY THE GAME, YOGI BERRA . . .

appeared in 21 World Series: 14 as a player, 5 as a coach, and 2 as a manager.

won 10 World Series as a player, more than anyone in baseball history.

won 3 Most Valuable Player (MVP) Awards (1951, 1954, and 1955) and never finished lower than 4th in the voting from 1950 through 1957.

was elected to 18 All-Star Games but played in 15 (1948–1962).

was inducted into the National Baseball Hall of Fame in 1972.

YOGI BERRA MUSEUM & LEARNING CENTER
yogiberramuseum.org

Although Yogi is no longer with us, his legacy lives on at the Yogi Berra Museum & Learning Center. Located on the campus of Montclair State University, the museum was built in 1998 as a place where the values that made Yogi a national treasure—perseverance, sportsmanship, respect, and excellence—are sustained for a new generation of learners and leaders. Every year, thousands of children and their families enjoy the museum's sports-based exhibits and programs, testimony to the fact that when it comes to Yogi and his standard for doing what was right, "it ain't over!"

BIBLIOGRAPHY*

Barra, Allen. *Yogi Berra: Eternal Yankee.* New York: W. W. Norton, 2009.

Bartlett, John. *Bartlett's Familiar Quotations.* 17th ed. Edited by Justin Kaplan. New York: Little Brown, 2002.

Baseball-Reference.com. "Yogi Berra." baseball-reference.com/bullpen/Yogi_Berra.

Berra, Yogi. *Yogi: It Ain't Over.* With Tom Horton. New York: McGraw-Hill, 1989.

———. "Yogi Berra." Interview. Academy of Achievement, Baseball Hall of Fame. New York, June 1, 2005. achievement.org/achiever/yogi-berra/#interview.

———. *The Yogi Book: "I Really Didn't Say Everything I Said."* New York: Workman, 1998.

———. *You Can Observe a Lot by Watching: What I've Learned About Teamwork from the Yankees and Life.* With Dave Kaplan. Hoboken, NJ: Wiley, 2008.

Berra, Yogi, and Ed Fitzgerald. *Yogi: The Autobiography of a Professional Baseball Player.* Garden City, NY: Doubleday, 1961.

Blount, Roy, Jr. "Yogi vs. Yogi." *Sports Illustrated,* October 1, 2015, pp. 48–55. First published April 2, 1984.

Burnes, Robert L. "My Friend Yogi." *Sporting News,* November 6, 1957, p. 11.

Carmichael, John P. "Hogan Isn't Done, Warns Little." *Toledo Blade,* April 23, 1954, p. 40. news.google.com/newspapers?id=PYlOAAAAIBAJ&sjid=ggAEAAAAIBAJ&pg=3406%2C3629240.

Chicago Daily Tribune. "East Chicago Is Beaten, 25–0, by St. Louis Legion." August 17, 1942, p. 20.

Coffey, Terry. "The Yankee Quipper." *The American Legion* 46, no. 4 (April 1999), pp. 28–30.

Daley, Arthur. "Innings and Outings of Spring Training." *New York Times Sunday Magazine,* March 20, 1955, p. 17.

———. "Our Boy, Yogi." *New York Times,* December 13, 1954, p. 38.

———. "Yogi and the Award." *New York Times,* November 14, 1951, p. 54.

DeVito, Carlo. *Yogi: The Life and Times of an American Original.* Chicago: Triumph, 2008.

Dickson, Paul. *Baseball's Greatest Quotations.* New York: Harper Perennial, 1991.

———. "Honoring Yogi Berra—What He Really Said." The National Pastime Museum, September 28, 2015. thenationalpastimemuseum.com/article/honoring-yogi-berra-what-he-really-said.

Drebinger, John. "Bombers Overcome Hassett Tars, 19–5." *New York Times,* April 8, 1947, p. 37.

———. "Boston's 3rd in 9th Beat Bombers, 5–4." *New York Times,* March 28, 1947, p. 30.

Gay, Jason. "The Extraordinary Journey of Yogi Berra." *Wall Street Journal,* September 23, 2015. wsj.com/articles/the-extraordinary-journey-of-yogi-berra-1443031345.

---

*Websites active at time of publication

Havemann, Ernest. "Why Pitchers Get Nervous." *Life*, July 11, 1949, pp. 71–77.

Jaffe, Jay. "Pantheon Player." *Sports Illustrated*, October 1, 2015, pp. 14–15.

Klingaman, Mike. "Yogi Berra Was Wonderful 'Unless You Were Batting,' O's Slugger Boog Powell Remembers. *Baltimore Sun*, September 23, 2015. baltimoresun.com/sports/bal-former-orioles-slugger-boog-powell-fondly-remembers-yogi-berra-20150923-story.html.

Liberman, Noah. *Glove Affairs: The Romance, History, and Tradition of the Baseball Glove*. Chicago: Triumph, 2003.

McCulley, Jim. "Yankees Rip A's 4–3, 7–4; 2 Rookies HR." *New York Daily News*, September 23, 1946.

McNeil, William F. *Backstop: A History of the Catcher and a Sabermetric Rating of 50 All-Time Greats*. Jefferson, NC: McFarland, 2005.

Mormino, Gary Ross. *Immigrants on the Hill: Italian-Americans in St. Louis, 1882–1982*. Urbana: University of Illinois Press, 1986.

New York News/Chicago Tribune Dispatch. "Berra a Yank Regular." *Chicago Daily Tribune*, March 11, 1947, p. 29.

Posnanski, Joe. "A Living Legend Even After He's Gone." *Sports Illustrated*, October 1, 2015, p. 67. First published July 4, 2011.

Schoor, Gene. *The Story of Yogi Berra*. Garden City, NY: Doubleday, 1976.

Serby, Steve. "Berra on Mantle, DiMaggio, Yogi-isms in Never-Published Q&A." *New York Post*, September 23, 2015. nypost.com/2015/09/23/berra-on-mantle-dimaggio-yogi-isms-in-never-published-qa/.

Shapiro, Ed, ed. *The Yale Book of Quotations*. New Haven, CT: Yale University Press, 2006.

Shapiro, Milton J. *Heroes Behind the Mask: America's Greatest Catchers*. New York: Julian Messner, 1968.

Sharkey, Joe. Jersey; Commencement Ain't Over Till It's Started. *New York Times*, May 19, 1996. nytimes.com/1996/05/19/nyregion/jersey-commencement-ain-t-over-till-it-s-started.html.

Smith, Lee. "The Greatest Catcher Who Ever Lived." *Weekly Standard*, September 24, 2015. weeklystandard.com/print/the-greatest-catcher-who-ever-lived/article/1035671.

Verducci, Tom. "A Great American Life." *Sports Illustrated*, October 1, 2015, pp. 9–13. First published September 23, 2015.

Ward, Arch. "First Cubs to Report Feb. 16 at Catalina." *Chicago Daily Tribune*, December 5, 1946, p. 57.

———. In the Wake of the News (column). *Chicago Daily Tribune*, November 22, 1951, p. H1.

Wind, Herbert Warren. "From the Hill to the Hall." *Sports Illustrated*, March 2, 1959, pp. 63–69.

Yogi Berra Museum and Learning Center. yogiberramuseum.org.

"I WANT TO THANK EVERYONE WHO MADE THIS DAY NECESSARY." —Yogi

ACKNOWLEDGMENTS

Thanks to the staff at the Yogi Berra Museum and Learning Center at Montclair State University in New Jersey for the tour, research materials, and review of the art and text.

—BR

"I REALLY DIDN'T SAY EVERYTHING I SAID." —Yogi

A NOTE ABOUT YOGI-ISMS

Yogi Berra's quotations, or Yogi-isms, are legendary. Original sources for his sayings are notoriously difficult to pin down. Many Yogi-isms seem to be original, but others may have been used by someone else first, then popularized by Berra. All of Yogi's remarks were unplanned and many were overheard in dugouts, locker rooms, golf courses, etc., so exact wording is often disputed. For example, is it *"When* you come to *the* fork in the road" or *"If* you come to *a* fork in the road" or "So? I don't hit with my face" or "So what? I never saw anyone hit with his face"? No one knows. Yogi's own memories of what and why he made some remarks changed over time. He was known to say, "I could've probably said that" or "Half the things I said, I never said them" as an answer to whether a quote was true or not. Any Internet search unfortunately will give you many sayings falsely attributed to Berra. So the main sources for the Yogi-isms in this book were *Bartlett's Familiar Quotations*, *The Yale Book of Quotations*, Paul Dickson's *Baseball's Greatest Quotations*, and a 1984 *Sports Illustrated* article by Roy Blount Jr. about Yogi's wise words and which ones were authentic. The best explanations for when and why Yogi made a remark can be found in *The Yale Book of Quotations*.

—BR

QUOTES ABOUT YOGI BERRA

He can walk into a ballpark filled with 60,000 people or a room filled with 40, and when they see him, they stand, and it's as though they are saying, "I like this guy. I want him to be my friend." If you don't like Yogi, you're un-American.
—Joe Garagiola, former St. Louis Cardinals catcher, announcer, and Yogi's childhood friend

To those who didn't know Yogi personally, he was one of the greatest baseball players and Yankees of all time. To those lucky ones who did, he was an even better person.
—Derek Jeter, former New York Yankees shortstop, five-time World Series champion

I don't care what team you play for or what team you root for, if you love baseball, then you love Yogi Berra.
—Jorge Posada, former New York Yankees catcher & Silver Slugger Award winner

Every person that met Yogi had admiration for his character and his heart.
—Reggie Jackson, rightfielder, member of the Baseball Hall of Fame

Every time I see him, I feel a little better about the human race.
—Bobby Brown, 3rd baseman, physician, and former American League president

He is the same today as yesterday as tomorrow. He is never late. He is never mean. And he never misses a Yankees game.
—Carmen Berra, Yogi Berra's wife

Yogi Berra was an American original—a Hall of Famer and humble veteran; prolific jokester and jovial prophet. He epitomized what it meant to be a sportsman and a citizen, with a big heart, competitive spirit, and a selfless desire to open baseball to everyone, no matter their background.
—Barack Obama, former U.S. President

SOURCE NOTES

Each citation indicates the first words of the quotation and its document source. The sources are listed either in the bibliography or below. All quotations are attributed to Yogi Berra except where noted.

"It was fun. . .": CNN video memorial, September 23, 2015. youtube.com/watch?v=2Yoys_D8FLQ.

"How do you like . . ." and "Closed . . .": Barra. p. 14

"We were overwhelming . . .": Barra, p. 317.

"When you come to a fork . . .": Bartlett, p. 814.

"a bum's game": Barra, p. 14.

"You can observe . . .": Bartlett, p. 814.

"In baseball, you . . .": same as above.

"If the world were perfect . . .": Berra, *The Yogi Book*, p. 52.

"Ninety percent of this game is . . .": Dickson, *Baseball's Greatest Quotations*, p. 44.

"What tree did . . .": DeVito, p.95.

"captain of the . . .": Berra, Fitzgerald, p. 96.

"He doesn't even . . .": Berra, Fitzgerald, p. 97.

"It's not too far . . .": Berra, *The Yogi Book*, p. 100.

"So? I don't . . .": Berra, *The Yogi Book*, p. 112.

"We made too many . . .": Dickson, *Baseball's Greatest Quotations*, p. 44.

"How can you think . . .": Bartlett, p. 814.

"How's the family . . .": Serby, website.

"Have a good . . ." and "Shut up! . . .": Barra, p. 112.

"What are you . . .": Klingaman, website.

"It's never happened in . . .": Barra, p. 225.

"Hello, Yogi . . .": Blount, p. 48.

"It's so crowded . . .": Dickson, p. 44.

"If you can't . . .": Dickson, p. 43.

"It's déjà vu . . .": Dickson, p. 44.

"It ain't over . . .": Bartlett , p. 814.

"You've got to be careful . . .": Dickson, *Baseball's Greatest Quotations*, p. 45.

"the greatest catcher . . .": James, Bill, quoted in Gay, website.

"He's out there . . .": Wind, p. 65.

"I always thought the record . . .": Dickson, *Baseball's Greatest Quotations*, p. 42.

"I want to thank everyone . . .": Shapiro, *The Yale Book of Quotations*, p. 58.

"I really didn't say . . .": Berra, *The Yogi Book*, p. 9.

"He can walk . . .": Garagiola, nj.com/sports/ledger/ izenbergcol/index.ssf/2015/09/why_yogi_berra_was_ so_loved_he.html.

"To those who . . .": Jeter, mlb.com/players/jeter_derek/ article.jsp?ymd=20150923&content_id=151203080.

"I don't care . . .": Posada, mlb.com/players/jeter_derek/ article.jsp?ymd=20150923&content_id=151203080.

"Every person that . . .": Jackson, nydailynews.com/sports/ baseball/yankees/sports-world-reacts-death-yogi-berra-90-article-1.2372132.

"Every time I . . .": Brown, quoted in Verducci, Tom. "A Great American Life." *Sports Illustrated*, October 1, 2015, p. 11. First published September 23, 2015.

"He is the . . .": Berra, Carmen, quoted in Posnanski, Joe. "A Living Legend Even After He's Gone." *Sports Illustrated*, October 1, 2015, p. 71. First published July 4, 2011.

"Yogi Berra was . . .": Obama, cnn.com/2015/09/23/ politics/yogi-berra-jeb-bush-hillary-clinton-donald-trump-tribute/.

PICTURE CREDITS

To Danny, my own #8 —*BR*

For the families who live and have lived on The Hill—*TW*

Calkins Creek
An Imprint of Highlights
815 Church Street
Honesdale, Pennsylvania 18431
calkinscreekbooks.com
Printed in China

ISBN: 978-1-62979-824-0
Library of Congress Control Number: 2018940081

First edition
10 9 8 7 6 5 4 3 2 1

Design by Barbara Grzeslo
The text is set in Futura Medium
The title and quotes are hand-lettered by David Coulson.
The illustrations are done in acrylic on Bristol paper.